A Journey Toward Kingdom Living

40 Devotionals Inspired by the Work of Dallas Willard

Nathan Gibbs, David Jentsch, & Adam Jones

Introduction

A Journey Toward Kingdom Living was written and compiled as part of a project for a class taught at Baylor University's George W. Truett Theological Seminary. This class, taught by Dr. R Robert Creech, took students through several works of Dallas Willard. First the class read the biography *Becoming Dallas Willard* by Gary Moon. This biography gave us valuable insight into the life of Dallas Willard better enabling us to understand his writings. Next, we read *The Divine Conspiracy, The Spirit of the Disciplines,* and *Renovation of the Heart.*

Our desire in writing this devotional was to highlight some of the insights and lessons that Willard was so gracious to share with people in his books and turn them into practical daily devotionals to help point readers forward on their journey toward kingdom living. It is important to remember that this devotional is not a forty-day recipe for a transformed life; that requires a lifetime of pursuing Christ. Our hope is that this book will serve as a resource to help guide that pursuit over the course of forty days.

Each devotional includes a quote from Dallas Willard. For the sake of saving space, each book title was abbreviated as follows: BDW – *Becoming Dallas Willard*, DC - *The Divine Conspiracy*, SD – *The Spirit of the Disciplines*, RH - *Renovation of the Heart*, HG – *Hearing God*, GO – *The Great Omission*. After each quote, there is a Bible verse or passage included. Each verse is quoted from the New Revised Standard Version. Then follows a small lesson, some questions for further understanding, and a written prayer.

We want to encourage readers to use these devotionals as a place to start. Meditate and pray on each devotional. Ask God to speak to you through each one. We believe it would be beneficial to keep a journal while working through this book. Be mindful not to treat these devotionals as an item to check off each morning, rather as an opportunity to interact with God.

Whether you find these devotionals helpful or not, we hope that you will pick up some of Dallas Willard's books to read so that you can be formed by his teachings; just as we have been.

Blessings as you begin this journey,

Nathan, David, & Adam

Available to All

"The gospel of the kingdom is that no one is beyond beatitude, because the rule of God from the heavens is available to all. Everyone can reach it, and it can reach everyone." (DC 122)

"Blessed are the poor in spirit, for theirs is the kingdom of heaven." Matthew 5:3

The beauty of the gospel is that the kingdom of heaven is now available to everyone. We, the broken sinners, are welcomed into life with God the most high and allowed to participate in the rule of heaven. We know this truth in our head, but it is far too easy for us to walk through our week as if it were not so. We shout at the car who cuts us off in traffic, mutter insults under our breath when we pass a drug addict, condemn criminals to hell when we see them on the news.

This was not the example demonstrated by Jesus while he walked on Earth with us. To the diseased, he said blessed. To the tax collectors, blessed. To the Pharisees, blessed. None were too far gone, none were rejected. We are to strive to be like Jesus. In order to do so it is pivotal that we recognize the reality that the kingdom of heaven is available to all.

So, to whom is the kingdom of heaven available to? The preacher, the doctor, and the teacher, blessed. The banker, the politician, and the salesman, blessed. The thief, the gossip, the murder, even they too have the kingdom available to them. How do we communicate the availability of heaven to those we look down upon and despise? It is in showing grace, compassion, and care to those who do not deserve it, that we are able to show that the grace of God is available to them.

May we look to the gospels and be moved to not only believe the teachings of Jesus but follow the example that he set. The gospel can reach everyone; let us partner with our savior and share it with those around us.

Questions for Understanding

Who have you ignored and deemed unworthy of receiving the gospel?

Imagine what your life would look like were you to treat all those around you as sons and daughters of the King of kings.

Prayer

Redeeming Savior, who has made your kingdom available to us; remind us today that we are unworthy of your grace and love, so that we might pursue the lost who are walking amongst us to the glory of your name; through Jesus Christ our Lord. Amen.

Comfort

"Those poor in spirit are called 'blessed; by Jesus, not because of they are in a meritorious condition, but because, precisely in spite of and in the midst of their ever so deplorable condition, the rule of the heavens has moved redemptively upon and through them by the grace of Christ." (DC 102)

"'But Zion said, "The Lord has forsaken me, my Lord has forgotten me." Can a woman forget her nursing child, or show no compassion for the child of her womb?" Isaiah 49:14-15

Suffering is an inescapable reality. Although dependent on our life circumstances, we all have experienced suffering at one time or another. Even if our existence has been a charmed one up to this point, it is only a matter of time before hardship hits. When confronted with suffering we react in a whole host of different ways. Some poor, others better.

Often times, the bitter fruits of suffering can seem insurmountable as we struggle through the pain. It is a natural and common reaction to assume God has forgotten us in our suffering. We need not feel guilty at such feelings as they are natural and often lead to a deeper faith. Jesus was well-aware of the toll that suffering takes on us; he pronounced a blessing on those who were poor in spirit. Life had beaten them down, they had been good people, but life cared little it seemed. In his blessing, Jesus was not approving of their situation, rather he was pointing out the redemptive work that was already underway. Their poor condition was not good in itself; rather, what was good was God's actions toward them. His Kingdom had come, and every tear was to be wiped away.

God does not desire us to be downtrodden or abandoned. We are designed to be his children who enjoy him forever. God allows us to experience the difficulties of life for reasons we don't know. What we can know, however, is God's steadfast goodness toward us during our pain, knowing that he is and always will be with us wiping away every tear.

Questions for Understanding

How are we to prepare for suffering that is surely coming our way?

What suffering have you experienced? And what have you learned about God through it?

Prayer

O Divine Comforter, we thank you for your gentle hand that wipes away our tears. We ask that you prepare us in Christ-likeness knowing in you we can be safe from the storm. Let us not turn from you in trials, Father, instead let us turn to you as our only haven. Renew us, good Savior, in your image. Amen.

God is Near

"This ill-advised attempt to make God near by confining him to human hearts robs the idea of his direct involvement in human life of any sense. Ironically it has much the same effect as putting God in outer space or beyond. It gives us a pretty metaphor but leaves us vainly grasping for the reality." (DC 74-75)

"Indeed, those who are far from you will perish; you put an end to those who are false to you. But for me it is good to be near God; I have made the Lord God my refuge, to tell of all your works." Psalms 73:27-28

I remember very clearly when I first asked God "into my heart" as a child. I also remember my motivation for doing so; I literally wanted to see God fly into my stomach and move through my body and wind up in my heart. Much to my disappointment, none of this transpired. I was disappointed and convinced that God was not real. To me, God was not dissimilar to Santa Claus or the Easter Bunny, and when I prayed the "magic prayer" and nothing happened, I proved to myself God was not real.

This is part of the issue with our metaphor of "having God in our hearts". "'In my heart' easily becomes 'in my imagination'" (DC 74). We would be better to speak of God being present, rather than hidden in our hearts or anywhere else. God is near. God is here. Any attempt to place God somewhere other than right with us serves to ignore his involvement in our daily lives.

God desires to be known, it is in his nature as a loving God. God does not depart when we go to sleep at night, only to arrive again once we wake. He is ever-present. Practicing seeing God in the world around us enables us to grow in intimacy with him. Look for God today.

Questions for Understanding

Where do you picture God residing?

If you saw God all around you, how might your life look different?

Prayer

Ever-present God of creation, thank you for choosing to be present with us so that we need not go through this life alone. I ask that you make your presence known to me today, let me hear you in the wind and feel your hand guiding my steps in order that I may know you more. It is in the name of your son, Jesus Christ, I pray. Amen.

A Kingdom Ecology

"You cannot call upon Jesus Christ or upon God and not be heard. You live in their house, their echoes. We usually call it simply 'the universe.' But they fully occupy it. It is their place, their 'kingdom,' where through their kindness and sacrificial love we can make our present life an eternal life. Only as we understand this, is the way open for a true ecology of human existence, for only then are we dealing with what the human habitation truly is." (DC 32-33)

"For every house is built by someone, but the builder of all things is God." Hebrews 3:4

How are we to give an account of a given organism if we are not aware of its environment? Take for example a coral fish, they come in all shapes and sizes and if examined by themselves, we could know their weight, color, texture, and a whole host of other facts about them. It is true that these are of interest to many, but it would be wrong to think this is the whole story, for the obvious question remains—what does this animal do? In separating the fish from its environment our observations become too narrow. We would need to examine its environment to answer the truly important questions about the fish.

Function, you see, is rooted in one's environment, the fish's function is not only in its anatomy but also in its relation to the reality in which it finds itself. This is no less true for humans. We find ourselves in a world where we must act. The difficulty lies in how we should act, or what principles should govern our action. Philosophers from time past have been seeking to answer this enigmatic question, coming up with a whole host of answers ranging from hedonism to nihilism.

The Christian, however, finds themselves in a different world; one governed by a God who is not far off. Thus, the Christian's ecology is different from her secular counterparts' and must be mapped in order to discern how she is to live. Like the coral fish, she must determine her environment if she is to know her function.

Questions for Understanding

Consider for a moment your environment, not the one perpetuated by our so-called enlightened worldview, but the one where Christ is King, where His rule is perfect, and you are his servant and precious child. How would this affect your daily life? Would you live differently if you *really* believed this?

Prayer

Heavenly Father, we praise you for your goodness in creation, in that in you we may find our home. May we become aware of your presence with us. May we see in everything your handiwork. Let us not be drawn in to lies concerning who and what we are, and instead be drawn ever more into your tender love. Give us your Spirit, O Lord, to live according to your image, in that all we do will be for your glory. Amen.

Being at Home in God's Kingdom

"In order to become a disciple, then, one must believe in him. In order to develop as his disciple, one must progressively come to believe what he knew to be so. To enter his kingdom, we believe in him. To be at home in his kingdom, learning to reign with him there, we must share his beliefs." (DC 319)

"Believe me that I am in the Father and the Father is in me; but if you do not, then believe me because of the works themselves. Very truly, I tell you, the one who believes in me will also do the works that I do and, in fact, will do greater works than these, because I am going to the Father. I will do whatever you ask in my name, so that the Father may be glorified in the Son. If in my name you ask me for anything, I will do it." John 14:11-14

Belief in Jesus Christ and his life, death, and resurrection, is essential to enter into his kingdom. But when God brings us into his kingdom, we are not supposed to just stay at the entrance. God wants us to go further in to his kingdom so that we can become closer to him. How do we go deeper? By sharing the beliefs of Jesus, not just believing in him for the forgiveness of sins.

Jesus believed that the kingdom of God was present and should be lived in now. And because the kingdom is here, we must keep his commandments. Jesus' commandments originated from his belief about God's desire to have a relationship with humanity, and that this relationship starts now by obeying him. But it can become easy to divorce the life of Jesus from the teachings of Jesus.

As Dallas Willard so often points out, we are primarily concerned with getting saved and the rest is less relevant. Salvation is not just about getting into Heaven later but having a relationship with God now and forever. And if we want to engage with him, we have to know the core of Jesus' teachings. We have to share his beliefs. Why? Because it makes our faith real. It transforms us into Christ's likeness. When we believe what Jesus believed and practiced what he taught, we experience his kingdom in the here and now. He is no longer relegated to a deity that gets me into heaven, but as a present king who is truly present, relational, and loving. Even if he may not be perceptible, he is present. This is the heart of discipleship: being transformed into a person who loves God more and wants to follow him. That is how we reign with him. Why wait until Heaven when you can live this life now?

Questions for Understanding

In what areas of your life are you struggling to submit to Jesus and truly believe what he says?

What lies about yourself have you believed that contradict what Jesus believes about you?

Prayer

Almighty God, you crossed over into our world to establish your reign through your Son. Now you call us to reign with him. Make the truth of your Kingdom as taught by Jesus resonate within us and transform our hearts. Give us the strength and will to follow you and to abide in your kingdom now and act as citizens of your kingdom in everything we do. We pray in the name of your Son, our Savior Jesus Christ; who lives and reigns with you, in the unity of the Holy Spirit, one God, now and forever. Amen.

The Discipline of Dominion

"Our care about the extinction of species and our general feeling of responsibility and concern for the fate of animals, plants, and even the earth also speaks to this divine intention. Scientists talk easily and often of our responsibility to care for the oceans and forests and wild, living things. This urge toward such responsibility is, I think, only a manifestation of the imago Dei originally implanted in humankind and still not wholly destroyed." (SD 51)

"Then God said, 'Let us make humankind in our image, according to our likeness; and let them have dominion over the fish of the sea, and over the birds of the air, and over the cattle, and over all the wild animals of the earth, and over every creeping thing that creeps upon the earth.'" Genesis 1:26

Environmentalism raises red flags in many Christian circles. "If God gave people dominion over the earth, God gave people approval to use the earth as they see fit." But when God gave us dominion, he was not giving us permission to consume the earth's resources without any consideration of the consequences. He wanted us to participate in his work in creation.

The Creation stories in Genesis describe a God who brings order from chaos. Out of nothing, he creates something good. This is drastically different from the other creation myths of ancient civilizations. If bringing order from chaos and recognizing the goodness of creation are distinct qualities of our God, they should be distinct qualities in us as well because we are made in his image. That is why God gave humanity dominion over the earth.

Therefore, we should take care of creation. Even if it seems inconvenient. After all, if it did not require any level of personal sacrifice, it would not be a discipline.

There are two ways that we can change our lifestyles so that we can be involved with God's work in creation. First, we have to spend time in nature. Getting outside and breathing fresh air and experiencing nature first hand allows us to know the beauty of nature as a reflection of God's beauty. So take a hike, get in a kayak, set up a hammock, and be present with God in his creation. The second way to practice the discipline of dominion is by being environmentally conscientious. We consume the resources God gave us without considering the consequences. Mindless consumption harms the world God gave us to steward.

Learn the behaviors you can change. They may be in small ways like not using disposable water bottles or it may mean making drastic changes to your life. Listen to the Holy Spirit's guidance on this issue.

Questions for Understanding

What is a way that you can regularly spend time outdoors?

What can you do to help the environment?

Prayer

Maker of Heaven and Earth, thank you for giving us the gift of creation. You allow us to partner with you by bringing order to the chaos in anticipation for Christ's return when all things will be made new. Convict us of our wastefulness and transform us from consumers into people who are consumed by you. For it is in you we live and move and have our being. Amen.

Cost

"As has been said, 'He is not a fool who gives up what he cannot keep for the sake of what he can never lose.' The cost of non-discipleship would then be seen for what it is—unbearable. That is why one would become able to sustain cheerfully the much smaller 'cost of discipleship' to him." (RH, 57)

"The steadfast love of the Lord never ceases, his mercies never come to an end; they are new every morning." Lamentations 3:22-23

From the outside, Christianity looks like a drab system of rules and practices designed to control those who partake in them. It leads, so some claim, to a dull and dreary life filled with boring services void of fun. Those of us in the Church should not be surprised by such observations as we know we are predisposed to dislike such things. We have, of course, been redeemed and view things in a new light. We see not a drab system but one that is a vessel through which God has chosen to manifest himself. We see things as they truly are, unaltered by a sinful predisposition.

Those outside see discipleship as constricting, we see it as freeing. The cost of discipleship, as it turns out, is quite little compared to the cost of its absence. Non-discipleship is what is truly costly. It is filled with destruction as our life is dominated by sin. Even worse, this is often happening unbeknownst to the one being destroyed. They are being led down a path to darkness they declare to be light. This situation is surely much costlier than discipleship. The latter leads to a deep relationship with your creator, the former increased isolation and depravity.

As we are trained in Christ-likeness, we no longer see the disciplines as such, instead they simply become the way of life for a God-infused person. They will no longer be strange practices, instead they will be like breathing an involuntary act needed for survival.

Questions for Understanding

While being a Christian can be difficult at times, have you considered the pain of not knowing God?

What does it mean to count the cost in light of the price of non-discipleship?

Prayer

Father, we thank you for the easy burden you have given us. It is not heavy, Lord, but light, guiding us in your way and filling us with an overwhelming joy. We pray that we would count the cost of following you daily, and that you would grant to us a sound mind in our appraisal recognizing the dire price of not knowing you. We pray that our lives may reflect our position as disciples. Amen.

The Real Bargain

"Those who are not genuinely convinced that the only real bargain in life is surrendering ourselves to Jesus and his cause, abandoning all that we love to him and for him, cannot learn the other lessons Jesus has to teach us. They cannot proceed to anything like total spiritual transformation." (RH 66)

"If anyone comes to Me, and does not hate his own father and mother and wife and children and brothers and sisters, yes, and even his own life, he cannot be My disciple." Luke 14:26

Much has been made about the cost required to follow Jesus. People often reference the above passage in Luke; others may point to Jesus' interaction with the rich young ruler (Mt. 19:16-22) when thinking about this cost. And yes, it is true, following Jesus will cost us everything; however, in giving up everything, we receive the only thing that ever mattered.

We were made to walk through life with God. By taking up our cross and following Jesus we receive the life that we were intended to have all along. Then, as if life now with God was not enough, we are able to enter the gates of heaven and dwell with our creator for eternity.

This life is not free. The requirements run counter to what our culture tells us we ought to do with our lives in the pursuit of happiness. We must die to ourselves, serve others, and seek Christ above all things. But this gift of life with God is oh so sweet! It is far greater than any type of life which we could possibly plan for ourselves. We get to play a part in something so much greater than ourselves.

So, while the cost of following Jesus is steep, the cost of not doing so is even steeper. When measuring up the costs, life with God appears as the real bargain.

Questions for Understanding

What would walking through life with Christ and nothing else look like?

What are you still holding onto, what have you failed to surrender to God?

Do you trust that Jesus is worth it?

Prayer

Giving Father, who has offered us life eternal with you; reveal to me the things I am still holding onto. Help me to abandon my life in order that I may find true life in you, through the power of the Holy Spirit. Amen.

The Narrow Gate

"But the truth about obedience in the Kingdom of Jesus, as should be clear by now, is that it really is abundance. Kingdom obedience is kingdom abundance." (DC 276)

"Enter through the narrow gate; for the gate is wide and the road is easy that leads to destruction, and there are many who take it. For the gate is narrow and the road is harsh that leads to life, and there are few who find it." Matthew 7:13-14

"[T]he road is harsh that leads to life." This verse has never really made sense to me. Why would the life of abundance that Jesus offers, be found on a harsh road? Could painful struggle really be the life that Jesus invites us to walk into? The life of the Christian is perceived to be one of following rules and laws that serve to deny oneself of the pleasures that life has to offer. If this were the case, why would anyone desire the Christian life?

What we need to understand is the backwardness of our common perception of Christian obedience. Christian obedience is not done to please God or to try and attain some result. It is the result of a transformed heart. When we become Christlike, to follow the law of God becomes the natural desire of our lives. From this place, we feel conviction when we sin, not out of shame at not being enough, but because we know that our sin is counter to what God desires for us and we want nothing more than to be aligned with our maker.

Obedience of the law is predicated on love. We must know and believe that God loves us and knows what is best for us in order for us to desire to follow his laws. Obedience is the narrow gate. Though difficult, it leads to the only life worth living.

Questions for Understanding

Do you desire to follow the law of God? Why?

Do you have the confidence in Jesus necessary to be obedient?

Prayer

Good and gracious God; you are worthy of obedience, honor, and praise. I thank you, today, for loving us enough to give us to give instruction on how to live. Give me the confidence in you to desire to follow you obediently today. May obedience be the natural outpouring of my life, I pray this in the name of our savior, Jesus Christ. Amen.

On Eternal Practice

"Full participation in the life of God's Kingdom and in the vivid companionship of Christ comes to us only through appropriate exercise in the disciplines for life in the spirit." (SD 26)

"But he would withdraw to deserted places and pray." Luke 5:16

A friend comes to you frustrated. She explains to you that her current state is due to her recent adoption of playing the piano as a new hobby. She had previously watched a video of Vladimir Horowitz and resolved to play Shumann's Traumerei just as he did. She describes her attempt as an utter failure as her fingers failed to glide across the ivory and her eyes failed to understand the notes set before her. Fuming, she asks for your advice. You, whether a pianist or not, will find her frustration peculiar.

Why does she assume she is capable of being a master pianist so quickly? If anything, you will advise her to practice diligently and after years she may be able to achieve her goal. Your advice assumes a universal human axiom—practice makes perfect. We all know this, but when approaching spiritual matters, we assume such an axiom doesn't apply, as if the laws of human formation were suspended by God. This is often accompanied with an appeal to grace—salvation is by grace alone, not practice. Though true, this response is lacking as it ignores spiritual formation. God not only desires we be saved, but that we be made into his image. Both, of course, are fueled by God's grace, but, they still require human effort in the form of practices that will form us into Christlikeness.

Jesus, himself, continually withdrew to pray to his Father realizing his dependence on him. Just as we are saved by Jesus, we are called to live as he lived. This includes the practices that he employed. If we are to become like him, we must live like him.

Questions for Understanding

How have you thought about spiritual formation? Are the spiritual disciplines something you are aware of or practice?

What practices did Jesus employ that we should emulate?

Prayer

Divine Master, we thank you for your guidance, in that, you have not left us in the dark but have shown us the light. We ask that you would lead us in your way, not only in mind, but in practice. May our lives increasingly reflect that of your Son's. Amen.

Practice makes Practicable

Peter and the other disciples would not in their moment of need have the ability to stand fast in the confrontation with Christ's enemies. But had they watched and prayed, as they were advised, the requisite ability would have been there when it was needed. They would have been in a condition of body and mind to secure the Father's assistance to stand as firmly as Jesus himself did. (SD 151)

"Then he came to the disciples and found them sleeping; and he said to Peter, "So, could you not stay awake with me one hour? Stay awake and pray that you may not come into the time of trial; the spirit indeed is willing, but the flesh is weak." Matthew 26:40-41

Allen Iverson was being questioned by the press about his practice habits. Iverson was not interested in answering the question and replied, "We're talking about practice...Not the game, but we're talking about practice, man. I mean, how silly is that?"

Iverson, like so many of us, suffer from a cognitive dissonance that prevents us from seeing the relationship between practice and "the game." But practice is what enables us to perform when the time has come. Peter, John, and James learned that the hard way.

Admittedly I failed to connect the dots. While I was working at a very stressful and spiritually draining job, I could not understand why I could not embody Christlikeness and was often frustrated at the job and the people around me. But I wanted to be patient and kind and unbothered by petty things. But I could not make myself just be better.

Then I read this, and it clicked in my brain and resonated in my heart. If I want to depend on God during the difficult times and constantly love the people around me at work, I would need to submit myself to Christ all the time.

This is why practice is so important. If I am unable to follow the teachings of Christ in controlled environments where it's easy, then I will be unable to when things are outside of my control.

The spiritual disciplines are how we practice submitting to God. It may be something that seems as simple as watching and praying. As we continue the disciplines, we come to a place where it becomes our first instinct to rely on God and not on our own strengths. We just need to surrender and follow. When we do that, our practices will become practicable.

Questions for Understanding

What things in your life you need to practice spiritual disciplines in order to prepare for?

How can you create an environment where you can practice the disciplines in order to prepare yourself for the "game"?

Prayer

Loving Father, you watch over us and guide us like a shepherd does for his sheep. Instill in us the determination to practice our faith constantly in order that we can glorify you when our faith is tested. In the name of Jesus Christ, your only Son and our Lord, we pray. Amen.

Your Best Life Now

Jesus' teaching does not lay out safe generalizations by which we can engineer a happy life. Instead, it is designed to startle us out of our prejudices and direct us into a new way of thinking and acting. It's designed to open us up to experience the reign of God right where we are, initiating an unpredictable process of personal growth in vivid fellowship with him. (SD 205)

The thief comes only to steal and kill and destroy. I came that they may have life, and have it abundantly. John 10:10

America loves the idea that Jesus came to teach how to live a happy life. Entire shelves in bookstores are dedicated to Christian self-help books filled with axioms and aphorisms. And we eat it up because we want to believe that if we just do what Jesus says, we'll be happy, successful, socially accepted or financially secure. We want the good life. Instead of giving us the wealth of kings and queens, Jesus taught how we can be under the reign of the good King.

Francis Thompson understood this. Thompson was a poet and homeless opium addict in Victorian era London. When Thompson met Jesus, he did not receive the keys to a castle. God didn't instantly cure him of a dependence on Opium. But Jesus showed him the kingdom of God on earth: a kingdom that was not distant, but accessible. He documents this experience in his poem *In No Strange Land:*

O world invisible, we view thee,

O world intangible, we touch thee,

O world unknowable, we know thee,

Inapprehensible, we clutch thee!

...
But (when so sad thou canst not sadder)
Cry;—and upon thy so sore loss
Shall shine the traffic of Jacob's ladder
Pitched betwixt Heaven and Charing Cross.

Yea, in the night, my Soul, my daughter,
Cry,—clinging to Heaven by the hems;
And lo, Christ walking on the water,
Not of Gennesaret, but Thames.[1]

That is the good life that Jesus promises. A good life which is good because God is present and reigning on earth and has made away for us to have a relationship with him.

Question for Understanding

What false ideas about the good life Jesus promises do you have?

Prayer

Gracious King, you have brought down your kingdom so that we might have the good, abundant life you promise. May we allow ourselves to yield to your teachings as revealed by your son Jesus Christ. And may the Holy Spirit enable us to obey. To him who is able to do infinitely more than we can ask or imagine we pray. Amen

You Can't God Your Own Way

"We are our own god, and our god doesn't amount to much." (RH 56)

When the people saw that Moses was so long in coming down from the mountain, they gathered around Aaron and said, "Come, make us gods[a] who will go before us. As for this fellow Moses who brought us up out of Egypt, we don't know what has happened to him." Exodus 32:1

We often judge the Israelites for making a golden calf right after God led them out of Egypt. "How could they just forget about God when they just crossed the red sea?" And we think to ourselves, "I would never make the same mistake they did!" But eventually we toss in our gold to construct an idol. I would wager very few of us have shrines in our homes dedicated to ourselves. We do not expect people to pray to us or claim to harness any supernatural power. And we certainly would never make sacrifices to ourselves for a bountiful harvest.

Even though we don't fit the description for most idols in the Bible, we still make ourselves into the idols of our hearts. We live and die for ourselves. We think that we can meet all of our needs for success, love, and security. This leads us to declare independence from God. Furthermore, whenever we sin, it is because we have elevated ourselves in our hearts to deity status. We prioritize what we want for ourselves over what God wants for us.

Fundamentally the issue is a lack of trust. Like the Israelites, we fail to see how God has been consistently faithful to us, so we attempt to follow our hearts and do what we think is best. Even if it means ignoring God.

But this is a path that is fruitless; we don't have the power that God has. Which is why we must tear down the idols of self and worship God. His way is the way that leads to peace, joy, and hope. He is the fountain of living water from which we can drink and be satisfied. If we drink from any other fountain, we will leave with a bitter aftertaste and an exacerbated thirst.

Questions for Understanding

In what areas of your life are you worshiping yourself above God?

How can you become more dependent on God?

Prayer

Faithful God, you alone are worth worshiping. Help us become more dependent on you and chase us down when we follow our own ways instead of following you. Give us love, you who are love. Give us peace, you who are peace. Amen.

Fallen Grace

"This fact of God's care and provision proves to all that no human condition excludes blessedness, that God may come to any person with his care and deliverance." (116, DC)

Blessed be the God and Father of our Lord Jesus Christ, the Father of mercies and the God of all consolation, who consoles us in all our affliction, so that we may be able to console those who are in any affliction with the consolation with which we ourselves are consoled by God. 2 Corinthians 1:3-4

One fall evening towards the end of my time in high school, I found myself standing over the twisted remains of the vehicle I had been riding in just minutes before. As I stood in shock observing the mangled machine, I felt the weight of my choices. I had chosen to get into a vehicle with a drunk driver; I had chosen to abuse the trust of those who loved me by living irresponsibly. Soon, I was facing those very people, admitting to all the horrible things I had been doing.

Up to this point, God and faith were noticeably absent from my life, and after experiencing what has been the lowest point of my existence, I assumed God would have nothing to do with me. Before, I had rejected him, now he would reject me. Yet, as I would come to learn, God's love was just beginning to take root in my life. Indeed, four years later, I would become a Christian. If it had not been for that fateful October evening I would have continued to ignore God, growing increasingly apart from him. In his grace, however, God allowed me to reap the fruits of my living. I was faced with reality, no more grand illusions. Reality, of course, was painful as I felt useless; a creature God could never love.

It was my darkest time to be sure, but it was only in the dark that I was able to see the divine spark. In a strange turn of events, I needed destitution in order to see God. Comforts could not do it; no amount of self-esteem could have either. God did not allow me to fall as an act of punishment, rather it was a colossal act of grace. God is with us in our best moments, but it is in our worst that the divine warmth draws even closer, reminding us we are forever his children and will not be excluded from his love.

Questions for Understanding

What destitute experiences can you look back on and see God's work?

How did God comfort you then and how is he comforting you now?

Prayer

Loving Father, we thank you for your faithfulness to us in that while we were still sinners you died for us. We pray that you would not let us stray from you, O Lord, and instead by your Spirit draw us ever closer to you. Suffer us not to be separated from you. Teach us to trust your guiding hand in the good times and the bad, knowing that you are always working for our good. Amen.

For the Lord

"If we restrict our discipleship to special religious times, the majority of our waking hours will be isolated from the manifest presence of the kingdom in our lives... Our time at work will turn out to be a "holiday from God."" (DC 287)

"Whatever your task, put yourselves into it, as done for the Lord and not for your masters." Colossians 3:23

One of the greatest temptations in Christianity is to box God into one or two days a week while we are at church. We go to church to make ourselves feel good and then we return to the normal stresses of our lives and live as though we are in control of our work week. This is not what unity with Christ looks like. A married person is not married for only one day a week nor does a married person wake up and decide if they are going to love their spouse that day. Why then do we approach our relationship with Christ in this way?

When we commit our lives to God, we do not commit just one part, but all of it. This includes our Monday through Saturday. Whether you work, go to school, take care of children, or are retired, those hours are to be dedicated to the Lord. We are called to prepare that expense report as if for the Lord, study for that exam as if for the Lord, and change that diaper as if for the Lord.

Doing our jobs as if they were done for the Lord is the best way to bring joy to work that may otherwise seem monotonous, for "the joy of the Lord is your strength" (Neh 8:10). God is not only at work on Sundays, he is active even while we sleep. May we live our daily lives in discipleship to the Lord.

Questions for Understanding

What would it look like to do your job as if you were doing it for the Lord?

What area of your life have you yet to surrender to God?

Prayer

Joyous creator; thank you for giving us a life to be lived. Teach us to serve you in everything that we do, in the big things in the little may we bring glory to your name. We ask this in the great name of our savior, Jesus Christ. Amen.

Beyond Fruit

"What God gets out of our lives—and, indeed, what we get out of our lives—is simply the person we become." (DC 250)

"I will put my law within them, and I will write it on their hearts; and I will be their God, and they shall be my people." Jeremiah 31:33

The age old story lies freshly on our ears as we depart from our time-honored place in the third pew from the back on the left-hand side of the sanctuary. We smile as the subtle joy that always seems to accompany God's saving grace floods our souls. We know the story by heart—God's love has prevailed over our sinfulness and we have been forgiven. The work is done, our blessed Savior testified as he hung on the tree.

Yet, is this it? Is God done with us? Has he wiped us clean only to leave us the same as we were, ready to be bedraggled once more? Surely not! No, he was forgiven us for a purpose. It is the means not the end of God's work. God is seeking redemption made possible because of his forgiveness. We are to be made new creatures, the very ones God conceived of in our creation. The distortions of sin and death are to be no more, we are to be brought unto fullness of life. The fruits of this will be many to be sure. We may feed thousands, clothe even more, or share the gospel with indomitable fury.

We will transform the world as God's Kingdom agent, conspiring against the forces of evil. Still, these are not the end for God or us. They are simply fruits. The person we become is God's prize. To be as God intended is his wish for us, nothing more, nothing less. To will as he wills, to see as he sees. There is no greater purpose.

Questions for Understanding

How have you thought of God's desire for your life? What have you thought God wanted out of you?

What practices can you engage in to grow into the person God desires you to be?

Prayer

Divine Potter, we thank you for your great patience and mercy. We ask that you mold us according to your will so that we may fulfill our created intent. Guide us in your ways, Lord, do not leave us in our old habits but transform them. Show us our role in this process, that we may, by your grace, participate in your glorious redemption project. Amen.

The Inner Cup

"It is the inner life of the soul that we must aim to transform, and then behavior will naturally and easily follow. But not the reverse." (DC 144)

"First clean the inside of the cup, so that the outside also may become clean." Matthew 23:26

You hear a clicking noise coming from the engine and immediately pull over and inspect the situation. After a period of analysis, you reach your solution. You go the backseat, find the jack and lug wrench, and go to work replacing your back left tire. At this point, you may be wondering what it is that you (or the fictional you) is doing. The story, like bad arithmetic, doesn't add up.

Even the most inept mechanic would know that an engine problem would not be solved by replacing a tire. Such absurdity is obvious to anyone, yet, to be candid, this is exactly what we do when attempting any sort of behavioral change. We have an issue of character which we would like to change but instead of addressing the root cause of the issue, we change something external. We, like the fictional you, change the tire in an attempt to fix the engine.

Focusing on the externalities is easy and requires little effort. Character change, however, requires great amounts of effort enacted and fueled by the grace of God. Jesus understood this in his critique of the Pharisees who were obsessed with externalities. They, to use our above passage, were concerned with the outer cup instead of the inner. We, of course, know that it is the inner cup where the water lies thus keeping it clean is of much more importance than the outer.

Character is the inner cup, it cannot be cleaned by wiping the outer portion. Jesus promises us his Spirit would indwell us, a process of inner transformation. Surely, this is a great act of grace, nevertheless, it is one that we must be involved in. We must repair the engine, the inner cup, not the outer, in full assurance that God is already there doing the cleansing.

Questions for Understanding

How have you attempted spiritual transformation? Have you focused on your inner or outer life?

What practices aim at inner transformation?

Prayer

Divine Healer, we praise you for your Spirit that indwells us. In the riches of your grace you have poured out yourself upon us. We ask, O Lord, that you would lead us to true character transformation into Christ-likeness. We pray that you would expose the externalities as inefficacious and lead us into practices that join the good work you are doing within us. Amen.

It's Not What You Know, It's Who You Know

"Knowledge" in biblical language never refers to what we today call "head knowledge," but always to experiential involvement with what is known--to actual engagement with it. (RH 51)

"Then Jesus said to the Jews who had believed in him, "If you continue in my word, you are truly my disciples; and you will know the truth, and the truth will make you free." John 8:31b-32

So much of children's ministry is dedicated to making sure the kids know the facts. They need to have the right answers, they need to memorize the verses to get the candy, they need to find Scripture passages faster than the other children their age, and the four step journey to salvation. As they transition into adolescence, they are taught new things: why they need Jesus, how to spread the Gospel on campus, and whether or not they should date.

The cycle continues when these people reach adulthood. We have been trained to think that the way to have a relationship with God is simply by knowing the right things. The church is full of Christians who know all of the Bible stories but never grow because they relegate knowledge to the head. We miss the point.

I know, because I did the same thing for a long time. I thought my knowledge about God in my head would allow me to coast through Christianity. But even though I kept learning more about my faith, I did not really experience God working in my life because my heart was hard.

Head knowledge is possible without Jesus Christ but is insufficient. We have to recognize that it is not enough to just have head knowledge. We need the knowledge about

God that only comes through engaging with God. Do not let your faith become a list of facts or Bible trivia. Engage in a personal relationship with God.

If God wanted people to only have a head knowledge, he would not have sent his Son, God Incarnate, to dwell among us and demonstrate that an experiential life with God is possible. But he came so that we may know him by experiencing and engaging with him.

Questions for Understanding

Is there a big difference knowing about God and knowing God?

How do we gain experiential knowledge about God?

Prayer

Immortal, invisible God, thank you for dwelling among us so that we might know you. Help us experience and be engaged with you at every moment, so that you will become the focus of our lives and the foundation of all of our knowledge. In the name of Jesus Christ, the Word made flesh, we pray through the Holy Spirit. Amen.

To Learn is to Change

"The aim of the popular teacher in Jesus' time was not to impart information, but to make a significant change in the lives of the hearers." (DC 112)

"Everyone who does not abide in the teachings of Christ, but goes beyond it, does not have God; whoever abides in the teaching has both the Father and the Son." 1 John 1:9

When we think of our school systems, we often think of students as information containers. The teacher works hard to impart knowledge to the students; they, in turn, take notes and study in order to reproduce the information on an exam. This is what learning is to us, essentially a transfer of knowledge.

Jesus, as the greatest teacher to ever live, taught in a way that would have a tangible influence on the life of the hearer. There was no need for the students of Jesus to take notes or record his message; and Jesus did not have to test his students later to see if they remembered what he said. Simply by looking at their lives, Jesus knew if his hearers had learned.

This is why the greatest Christian apologetic is not some sermon or book, it is living an authentic Christian life. When we, as Christians, live faithfully to the teachings of Jesus, people's lives are impacted rather than their heads. They no longer need to write down three sermon points, they simply are affected by our fruit.

Questions for Understanding

If Jesus were to look at your life, would he say you have learned what he taught?

What about your daily life is different because of your walk with Christ?

Prayer

Beautiful teacher, thank you for the wisdom and instruction you have given us, so that we need not figure out how to live on our own. I pray that you would teach me so that my life and heart may be transformed, that I may live and love like Jesus; in the great name of the Father, Son, and Holy Spirit. Amen.

I've Got a Bad Feeling About This...

"Feelings are a primary blessing and a primary problem for human life. We cannot live without them and we can hardly live with them. Hence, they are also central to spiritual formation in the Christian tradition. In the restoration of the individual to God, feelings too must be renovated: old ones removed in many cases, or at least thoroughly modified, and new ones installed or at least heightened into a new prominence." (RH 117)

"Since, then, you have been raised with Christ, set your hearts on things above, where Christ is, seated at the right hand of God. Set your minds on things above, not on earthly things. For you died, and your life is now hidden with Christ in God." Colossians 3:1-3

I have been told for most of my life that exercise makes people feel good. I didn't believe it because I didn't believe it would work for me. My wrong feeling was that I was not the perfect physical specimen, exercising would only shame me and make me feel worse. I had these feelings even though nobody had ever shamed me for exercising. The way for me to overcome this harmful feeling was by having a new feeling installed. I exercised when I didn't feel that it would make me feel good. Now on difficult days, I look forward to exercising because I have experienced that it makes me feel good.

I am a fairly sensitive person and I have never been able to fully just ignore my feelings, although I wish I could. But fortunately, as we grow and are formed by the Holy Spirit, our feelings do not go out of the process untouched. Christian growth does not require or encourage a person to become detached and emotionless. Jesus was constantly moved by his feelings. He was angry, he was distraught, he was joyful, and he was tired. But his supreme feeling is that he is a beloved child of God. This is the feeling that needs to be heightened to prominence in us. Then other feelings will be shaped by the constant feeling of being God's beloved child.

The feeling will not come in an instant but is something that takes time to sink in. The feeling may be installed through counseling, prayer, discipline, study, worship, medicine, or some other way. I wish it was easy, and I know you may feel discouraged. But when discouragement hits, do not ignore it. Recognize the feeling and remind yourself that you are a child who is fully loved by God and feel that love.

Questions for Understanding

What are the unhealthy ways that you deal with your feelings?

What false feelings do you have about yourself?

Prayer

O God who is slow to anger and abounding in love, you are not like the stone idols that feel nothing. You have given us feelings to glorify you. Help us be controlled by the feeling that we are your children. Expunge the lies that make us feel unloved. In the name of Jesus Christ, the full revelation of God, we pray. Amen.

Hear and Obey

"Hearing God – as a reliable, day-to-day reality for people with good sense – is for those who are devoted to the glory of God and the advancement of his kingdom. It is for the disciple of Jesus Christ who has no higher preference than to be like him." (HG 70)

"Let anyone with ears to hear listen"! And he said to them, "Pay attention to what you hear; the measure you give will be the measure you get, and still more will be given you."
Mark 4:23-24

"God has never spoken to me." This complaint brings with it doubt to the Christian who says it. Doubt about their salvation and doubt about the reality of God. If you can honestly say that you have never heard God, then there are two questions that must be asked. The first is "are you tuned in to God?" We have all called out to a friend from across the room only to find them too focused on what they are doing to be able to hear us. It is not that we have not spoken to them, they simply were not paying attention.

The second question we need ask is "are you ready to act upon what God says?" When God "speaks it is to accomplish his good purposes in our lives and through his creation" (HG 70). Have you ever decided not to give someone your advice, because you knew that they would not take the advice? This is not to say that God cannot or will not speak to those who are not ready to hear; however, we ought to prepare ourselves to hear and obey.

God is speaking. Are you listening? We must prepare our hearts to listen and seek to hear his voice. Not for our own personal gain, but to bring further glory to our God who reigns supreme. Hear and obey.

Questions for Understanding

Do you hear from God?

Are you a ready to act on what God says?

Prayer

God on high; we thank you for being a conversational God, that you are willing to provide guidance and instruction for the advancement of your kingdom. Father, I ask that you prepare my heart to hear from you today, speak for your servant is listening. It is in your hallowed name we pray. Amen.

Eternal Life is for the Living

"When we examine the broad spectrum of Christian proclamation and practice, we see that the only thing made essential on the right wing of theology is forgiveness of the individual's sins. On the left it is the removal of social or structural evils. The current gospel then becomes a "gospel of sin management." Transformation of life and character is no art of the redemptive message. Moment-to-moment human reality in its depths is not the arena of faith and eternal living." (DC 41)

"I ask not only on behalf of these, but also on behalf of those who will believe in me through their word, that they may all be one. As you, Father, are in me and I am in you, may they also be in us, so that the world may believe that you have sent me." John 17:20-21

We think Jesus died only to get people into Heaven or to denounce social injustices. But if Jesus only came to forgive personal sins so people can go to Heaven, he wasted a lot of time doing his ministry. If he only came to address structural evils, he failed in his mission because he did not lead a moral crusade against the Romans like the Zealots wanted.

The Eastern Orthodox church uses the word *Theosis* to describe life with God. It is foreign not only because it is in a different language, but because the term is usually absent from American Protestant churches. So, what is *Theosis*? It is the process by which people have a relationship with God and become united with him. *Theosis* does not just happen in the afterlife, but it begins now.

We have an opportunity to become incrementally more intimate with the God who loves us. We can be one with God as Jesus was one with God. And he came to show us how because Jesus Christ is not only the full revelation of God, he is also the pinnacle of humanity.

Jesus did come to forgive individual sins and tear down systems of oppression, but these were just aspects his mission. He came to offer people eternal relationship with God, and that relationship begins in this life.

This means having hope for a life after death. It means correcting systematic injustices in the present life. But it also means that God cares about me all the time and wants me to constantly grow in my relationship with him right now. It means allowing every part of myself to be sanctified and consumed by the Holy Spirit. This is the way that leads to a life of joy and satisfaction that only comes by becoming united with God.

Questions for Understanding

Which Gospel of sin management do you associate with?

How would you live if you truly believed eternal life with God starts in this life?

Prayer

Everlasting God, it is in you we live and move and have our being. Transform us so that we become more united with you. Enable us to live our lives dedicated to you in this life as well as in the life to come. To you who are greater to do infinitely more than we can ask or imagine we pray. Amen.

Union with Christ

"In the progress of God's redemptive work communication advances into communion and communion into union. When the progression is complete we can truly say, "It is no longer I who live, but it is Christ who lives in me." (HG 155)

"The glory that you have given me I have given to them, so that they may be one, as we are one, I in them and you in me, that they may become completely one, so that the world may know that you have sent me and have loved them even as you have loved me" John 17:22-23

God desires for us to be in union with him. Unity is not simply a close relationship; it is more than that. Unity literally means the state of being one. How then are we to go from lost and apart from God to a union with God?

The path to union with God begins with communication. Communication is vital to our life with God, just as it is in any other relationship; however, communication is only a starting point. From here we progress to communion with God. Communion is the sharing of intimate thoughts and feelings. Once we have arrived at this point we can, again, progress to union with God. At this point, the relationship is transformed. It is no longer *my* feelings or desires, rather they are *our* feelings. Jesus said that, "The Father and I are one" (Jn 10:30).

This unity is precisely the type of relationship that we are called to have with the Lord. Our desire must be to die to ourselves in order to take on the desires of Christ. We were created with a purpose, which can only be found when we lose ourselves and enter into a union with Christ.

Questions for Understanding

Where are you on the progression toward unity with God?

What steps do you need to take in order to advance closer to total unity?

Prayer

Heavenly Father who has created us with the purpose of dwelling in union with you; help us to press into communication with you that we may become at one with you and your ways. Let your desires become our desires in order for us to play a part in the advancement of your kingdom. To you be the glory and honor and praise. Amen.

Imitation

"He does not call us to do what he did, but to be as he was, permeated with love." (DC 183)

"You shall be holy, for I the Lord your God am holy." Leviticus 19:2

Adorning many wrists and necklaces is the acronym WWJD–What would Jesus do? In this catchy phrase we find the predominant question many ask themselves when faced with a difficult decision. The thinking is that we should make our decisions like Jesus would. While this question is a good one, it misses the primary issue. It is concerned with action; that is, what we should do in a given circumstance.

Action, however, does not exist in a vacuum, instead it stems from the type of person we are–our character. Thus, when people become frustrated at their inability to do what Jesus did it is not because they are not trying hard enough, but that they are not the type of person who could act like Jesus on a regular basis. Action is not predicated on will power but in character, thus in order to do what Jesus did, we must become who Jesus is. How are we to be like God you may ask? The answer, I think, lies in the life that Jesus modeled for us. In taking on flesh, Jesus, like us, was subject to sin, therefore he was forced to subdue sin and defeat its hold on humanity. This was accomplished in his life as well as his death.

The practices he modeled for us serve as disciplines by which we can enact the rule of God in our hearts, leading to a transformed character. We will then be like Jesus, permeated with love; holy as he is holy.

Questions for Understanding

What spiritual disciplines can you engage in to become like Jesus?

What would it look like to live like Jesus in your life?

Prayer

Jesus Christ, our Lord and Savior, thank you for your life you have set before us, one of love and purity. We ask that your indwelling Spirit would continue to transform us and lead us unto wholeness. May we become like you so that we may live as you live. Amen.

Differing Yokes

"We who are saved are to have a different order of life from that of the unsaved. We are to live in a different 'world.'" (SD, 37)

"Do not remember the former things or consider the things of old. I am about to do a new thing; now it springs forth, do you not perceive it?" Isaiah 43: 18-19

Think for a moment of a yoke—yes, that heavy piece of wood that often dons the shoulders of an oxen. What is its purpose? Is it not to guide and control the powerful animal according to its wielder's good pleasure? Jesus uses a yoke as an analogy for life with him; he claims that his yoke is light and easy to bear as opposed to others which are heavy and all but unbearable.

Why, though, we may ask, did Jesus, the one who sets us free, use this image to describe his kingdom? Would it not have been better to claim following him would result in no yoke? Ultimate freedom? The answer, I think, lies in Jesus' fundamental assumption about humanity—we are always yoked. It is an inescapable reality in which we find ourselves, the only question is which yoke we will choose. You see, to follow Jesus is to choose a yoke that is wholly different than what the world has laid upon your shoulders.

For many onlookers, the yoke given by Jesus will appear far too heavy for their backs to bear, but you will feel its true weight. The world's yoke, conversely, will grow increasingly heinous to you. You will see that it was not made of wood but of iron. Jesus' yoke will guide you unto green pastures, while the world's to barren wastelands. In a paradox, the very device used to control will be used to set you free. Free to live in God's Kingdom, apart from the illusions of this world. You will, then, bear the yoke gladly, recognizing the goodness of its wielder.

Questions for Understanding

How would you describe Jesus' yoke compared to the world's?

What would it look like to take on Jesus' yoke? What would it look like to inhabit a different world as he did?

Prayer

Loving Guide, we thank you for your yoke that leads us unto straight paths away from evil. We ask that you would teach us to take fully your yoke and cast off that of the world. We pray for your Spirit's good work in us that we may inhabit a new world where your Kingdom is our daily reality. Amen.

Take it Easy

"And all of our lack of understanding doesn't cancel his offer for an easy yoke and a light burden, in which our souls can find rest. That offer, like his call to follow him, is clearly made to us here and now, in the midst of this life where we labor and bear impossible burdens and cry out for rest. It's true. It's real. We have only to grasp the secret of entering that easy yoke." (SD 3)

"For my yoke is easy and my burden is light." Matthew 11:30

I'm afraid to rest. Resting, to me, requires ignoring all the important things I need to do; and if I do not accomplish everything on my to-do list, the world will fall apart. Then, what does it say about me if I cannot do everything I need to do? I have a control problem, and chances are you do too. But Jesus offers a better way.

Even though there is an open invitation to cast our burdens on him, we do not accept his offer. We ignore it until we are at our point of greatest exhaustion. Until we reach that point, we rest in our own ways. What then, is the secret of entering the easy yoke? Living in the present, as Jesus demonstrated. This means a life of dependence on God, rather than on ourselves.

His burden is still a burden. Jesus does not mean that we do not have to work or that we can rest on our laurels. Easiness means that we do not have to rely on our own efforts to live under his yoke. Lightness means that we do not carry the burdens of life on our own because God gives us strength. So, what does dependence on God instead of self mean?

It means practicing spiritual discipline, even when it seems unpleasant or even useless. It means recognizing that I cannot function autonomously and asking my sisters and brothers for help. It means taking his commandments seriously and living as a citizen of the kingdom. It may mean something as simple as realizing that it is okay if I do not fulfill every expectation I put on myself. And that maybe the best thing is to turn off my phone and walk through the park.

Questions for Understanding

Where do you find your source of rest? Would you say that these sources of rest are restorative or just a way to relax?

What can you do today in order to take on the yoke of Jesus?

Prayer

Lord Jesus Christ, Son of God, thank you for your invitation to a new way of life. You provide a way for us to find rest for our weary souls. Give us the wisdom to choose your burden instead of our own. Give us the strength to live as you lived. In your name we pray. Amen.

Never Alone

"The fact that only God can take away our aloneness by his presence explains why the ultimate suffering and punishment is separation from the presence of God." (HG 44)

"Even though I walk through the darkest valley, I fear no evil; for you are with me; your rod and your staff – they comfort me." Psalms 23:4

In our age of technology, we are more connected to each other than ever before. We have the ability to see a friend on the complete other side of the globe with the push of a button. We type things and post pictures that are available to our friends instantly. Why then is loneliness still such a prevalent condition in our society? Might it be that these people's "experiences of alienation are rooted in their alienation from God (HG 46)?

Human beings do not have the capacity to fully care for and appreciate other humans. As hard as a parent may try, they will not be able to fix the pain and loneliness that their child will experience at some point in their life. So, what leads us to continue to pursue earthly cures to our loneliness?

God created us. He knows the things we need, both physical and emotional. After creating Adam, God recognized that, "it is not good that man should be alone" (Gen 2:18). We should enjoy the gift of community that God has given us; yet there will be times when our earthly community fails us, and we feel lost and alone. When this happens where to we look?

We ought to turn our hope to God for he has promised that he "goes with you; he will not fail you or forsake you" (Deut 31:6). In Christ we are never alone. When we are worried, he is there. When we feel alone, he is there.

When no one cares, he is there. Press into the presence of Christ and take comfort in his rod and staff.

Questions for Understanding

What do you do when you feel alone?

How would your life be different if you were so close to God that you were never alone?

Prayer

Our God who is with us, thank you for giving us the gift of your presence. May our feeling of loneliness serve as a reminder that we are never truly alone. In those moments remind us to be in communion with you. To you be the glory. Amen.

In the Flatlands

"We're encouraged somehow to remove the essence of faith from the particulars of daily human life and relocate it in special times, places, and states of mind. More and more we are realizing the enormity of this problem." (SD 28)

"Trust in the Lord with all your heart, and do not rely on your own insight. In all your ways acknowledge him, and he will make straight your paths." Proverbs 3:5-6

A common metaphor for the spiritual life is that a person will experience times in the "mountains" and in the "valleys." The mountains are the highpoints of spiritual life. The last night of youth camp, Baptism, Christmas services, and when God's answer to prayer is visible. We can also experience God in the valleys. One of times I felt God's love the most was in crisis because I was surrounded by people who loving me.

These highs and lows are real, but they are not the only experiences. Living in Texas, we don't have a lot of mountains or valleys. It is just flat. Even the hill country is flat. Life is the same way. We do not spend our lives at either side of an extreme. Most of our lives are spent in the in-between space. And our natural tendency is to just coast in the middle until we experience a drastic life experience that gives us a spiritual high or makes us feel discouraged. The omnipresence of God means he with us in the boring times, the average times, and the mundane times. He allows us to recognize his presence in every minute of every day.

In his book Present Perfect, Greg Boyd shares one of his practices for remembering God's presence in the flatlands of life. Many Christians are asleep spiritually and are unaware of the presence of God all around them. To combat this, he writes post it notes that say "Are you awake?" Meaning, are you awake to the presence of God all around you, submerging you in love?[2] I have taken up this practice and it helps me remember God in the mundane. I encourage you to take action to remember God in the mundane. Whether it is sticking post-it notes around or another method, delight in God's presence and love in the mundane parts of life. You do not have to be on a mountain or in a valley to find God: He is in the flatlands with you!

Questions for Understanding

Where are the places where you get caught in a rut of routine and forget God's presence?

Maybe post-it notes are not your thing. What is a practice that you can do to help you remember God in the most mundane parts of life?

Prayer

Omnipresent God, you are with us in every part of our lives. You never abandon us or forget us, even when you forget we are with you. Help us to remember your presence in every part of our lives. Wake us up so that we can see you at work all around us. Through the Holy Spirit, your presence with us now, we pray. Amen.

Fatherhood

"Always, we are simply children walking and talking with our Father at hand." (DC 241)

"So he set off and went to his father. But while he was still far off, his father saw him and was filled with compassion; he ran and put his arms around him and kissed him." (Luke 15:20)

We often find ourselves is messy situations. Life presents us with countless difficulties: sickness, death, pain, personal and financial struggles, and many others that are inescapable. Each occupies so much of our mental space as we either try to get through them or avoid them entirely. Our lives are consumed by a constant desire to avoid the inevitable. In this pursuit of security, we get caught up in the race of life and are distracted from what it is we truly are.

We are like the prodigal son who finds himself in a far-off country seeking the good life (Luke 15). Little do we know that our Father spends every waking moment looking off into the distance awaiting his beloved child's return. We are seeking security and life in all the wrong places, forgetting what it is we were made for. Like a rose cut off from the stem, we may be able to survive for a brief period, but it is not our nature. We are designed to be attached to the plant that has given us life. Once we realize this, we can, like the son, make our way back to the Father who embraces us not with condemnation but with love. It is then that we realize who and what we are.

We are simply, and always will be, God's children, leaning on him, learning from him, becoming like him. In his possession, the difficulties of life become no more, they are little more than bumps along the way into our Father's arms.

Questions for Understanding

What difficulties are you going through and how have you coped with them?

What would it be like to cast your burdens on to God, remembering he is your loving Father who cares more deeply than you can imagine?

Prayer

Father, thank you for your provision in that we can find our home in you. Though the trials of life will come, we reign triumphant with you. Teach us to trust in you despite the pain. Guide us unto you that we may feel your tender embrace like the prodigal. Let us grow continually aware of your presence with us. Let us remember you are a God who weeps. Amen.

The Discipline of Community

"That is the meaning of the church as the body of Christ, the members nourishing one another with the transcendent power that raised up Christ from the dead and is now flowing through each member to the others." (RH 186)

"All these were constantly devoting themselves to prayer, together with certain women, including Mary the mother of Jesus, as well as his brothers." Acts 1:14

Imagine being in the place of the disciples after the ascension of their beloved friend and savior. They had already lost him once to death and when he came back, they thought, "Jesus is back, and everything is okay!" But he had to leave again. But he promised that his Comforter, the Holy Spirit, would come and be with them. But they probably did not understand the concept. I imagine that even though they had hope because they had seen the resurrected Jesus, they probably were a little lost and confused. Without Jesus' physical presence, how could they still have hope?

They were able to still have hope because they were functioning as the physical presence of Christ. Jesus' followers met together and prayed. We have the same opportunity to be the presence of Christ for one another. And we have the presence of Christ with us, demonstrated in the love others have for us. One of my professors would always remind his class that there are no maverick Christians. Nobody can maintain their faith autonomously. We need to be sustained by God through his church.

By practicing love, we are the actual presence of God. It is not God's way of passing the buck so he does not have to love. He shows his love for us by giving us the capacity to love one another. Be encouraged to go deeper into your relationships with others as you strive to grow deeper in your relationship with God. Do not deprive yourself of the nourishment that comes by being connected to a church. If you have been a victim of toxic church communities, this will be especially difficult. But the burdens of this pain can be lifted from your shoulders by finding a loving community.

Questions for Understanding

Do you tend to avoid building relationships at church? If so, why?

What are the practical ways that you can become more connected to the body of Christ?

Prayer

O God, you have not created us to be alone, but to dwell in community as you dwell in a divine community as Holy Trinity. Let be facilitators of love for one another, reflecting and embodying the love that you have for all. Empower your church to nourish the faith of the communion of saints. May the fellowship of the Holy Spirit be with us all. Amen.

Grace Consumed

"We consume the most grace by leading a holy life, in which we must be constantly upheld by grace, not by continuing to sin and being repeatedly forgiven. The interpretation of grace as having only to do with guilt is utterly false to biblical teaching and renders spiritual life in Christ unintelligible." (RH 82)

"But by the grace of God I am what I am and his grace toward me has not been in vain. On the contrary, I worked harder than any of them – though it was not I, but the grace of God that is with me." Romans 5:10

Perhaps you have heard this common explanation of grace, "God's riches at Christ's expense." This is a biblically correct explanation of grace; however, it fails to explain how we interact with grace. What do we do with grace? Are we to simply pray a prayer, receive our grace and move on with our lives? Surely not! We recognize that we can do nothing to earn grace, but we should not confuse this to mean we are to passively wait to receive it.

Far too often, we try to understand God's grace in terms of the grace we give to others. When a child accidently spills their drink on the brand-new carpet, they need grace from their parent; or when a spouse forgets to get milk on a trip to the grocery store, they need grace. The grace we receive from God is different. It is not merely forgiveness or patience, it is God acting in our life to do what we cannot. Because we are sinners, every good or righteous thing we do is through the grace of God.

Dallas Willard famously said that "the true saint burns grace like a 747 burns fuel on takeoff (GO 62). It is by the grace of God that we can do any good at all. A proper understanding of God's grace enables us to not confuse effort with legalism. We are called to pursue Christ, and it is only by the grace of God that we are able to so.

Questions for Understanding

What is grace?

What is the connection between grace and effort in our pursuit of Christ?

Prayer

Giver of grace, we thank you for the salvific work of Jesus on the cross. Give us the grace to do good today, that we may participate in the kingdom work to which you have called us, in the name of our redeemer, Jesus Christ, Amen.

More than Forgiveness

"Why is it that we look upon our salvation as a moment that began our religious life instead of the daily life we receive from God." (SD 28)

"For if while we were enemies, we were reconciled to God through the death of his Son, much more surely, having been reconciled, will we be saved by his life." Romans 5:10

Jesus Christ died for our sins; through his death, our sins are forgiven. However, Christian life is about so much more than just the forgiveness of sins. When we minimize our salvation to merely the forgiveness of sins we neglect the life of Jesus, instead focusing solely on his death.

The Romans passage listed above states that we will be saved by his life. If we believe that our salvation comes from Jesus' death on the cross, how then can we be saved by his life? Jesus himself is the physical manifestation of God dwelling among us. Our God knew that we needed to understand what life *with* God is like. Through the incarnation of Jesus Christ, human kind was able to dwell with God. That is the message of the gospels; that we are invited to daily communion with God, our savior. We need not wait for heaven to enjoy his presence.

Through salvation we are able to associate with God, but we are not required to wait until our arrival in heaven to do so. Our salvation is the daily life we receive from God. Salvation includes forgiveness, but it is so much more.

Questions for Understanding

What does it mean to be saved?

How does your understanding of salvation impact your view of Christian life?

How do you talk about salvation?

Prayer

Beautiful Savior, thank you for the life of Jesus and his salvific work performed on the cross. Teach us how to walk with you, that we may be reminded our salvation is more than forgiveness; we ask this in the name of your son, our Lord Jesus Christ. Amen.

Active Grace

"The harmonization of our total self with God will not be done for us. We must act." (SD 68)

"Pursue peace with everyone, and the holiness without which no one will see the Lord." Hebrews 12:14

What is it about our understanding of grace that paralyzes us? We from a young age have been ingrained with ideas about God's grace. We learn that it is a free gift which we could never earn no matter how good we are. We are taught to receive this gift and give a statement of belief in its giver. At that moment, we are saved from the perils of hell and our name is written in the book of life.

After, we are rarely called to a different way of life. If we do live differently wonderful! Praise God! For his grace is sanctifying us. But, the last thing we are to do is engage in a disciplined life where we employ large amounts of effort, because this, we are told, is antithetical to grace. We are told we are trying to earn our salvation, instead of receiving it from God. Our understanding of grace, then, forces us into passivity lest we be called a heretic. But, as the writer of Hebrews commands, we are to pursue peace and holiness.

Pursuit is not a passive activity but a fiery, active one. We cannot pursue anything while paralyzed, rather we must take off with full speed after our goal. Grace, to be sure, is a gift, but it is one that should move us to action as it serves as our fuel. We must act by grace in order to grow into Christlikeness, God will not do this for us. It is up to us to make the decision to do so. God has given us the ability and the means, but he will not force us.

Questions for Understanding

Has the above description been your view of grace? If so, has it led to action or paralysis?

How are we to use grace as fuel instead of trying to earn favor from God?

Prayer

Oh Giver of grace, we thank you for your never-ending mercy towards us. We thank you that while we strayed from you, you never strayed from us. We ask that you would move us to action, not motivated by earning, but by your love and grace towards us. We pray that by your guidance we would pursue harmony with you. Amen.

Two Hearts

"To understand Jesus' teachings, we must realize that deep in our orientations of our spirit we cannot have one posture toward God and a different one toward other people. We are a whole being, and our true character pervades everything we do". (DC 232)

"With it we bless the Lord and Father, and with it we curse those who are made in the likeness of God. From the same mouth come blessing and cursing. My brothers and sisters, this ought not to be so." James 3:9-10

It is so easy to switch between a loving posture towards God and a posture of dislike towards one of his creation. I notice it the most in myself when I am driving. Especially driving in a major city. It is easy to have a loving posture towards God when I am listening to my worship music Spotify playlist but instantly take on a different posture towards that maniac in the Mazda who just cut me off while crossing over three lanes of traffic without a blinker.

We are not acting like a whole person when we treat God with love and treat people with contempt. We feel torn and may question ourselves. Do I have two hearts? The one who loves God and the one that hates people? We cannot compartmentalize our relationship with God apart from our relationships with other people. God created us to be whole people, we cannot bifurcate our hearts and deny people love while claiming to love God. We need to love others with the same love that God has for them.

Jesus is the example of what it looks like to live and love holistically. Jesus was a completely whole person. He did not put on a different persona. He did not submit parts of his life to God and separate that from the rest. This is seen in his interactions with people. He would never tell his disciples, "I really hate these sinners" before having dinner with them. He did not even think dualistically. When he was talking to the tax collectors and prostitutes, his kindness and love was not a performance, but was congruent with his innermost self. Everything he did came from a place of sincere love. And he invites us to be transformed by the Holy Spirit, so we can love the same way.

Questions for Understanding

What parts of your life do you find yourself becoming routinely frustrated, angry, or contemptuous towards people?

What practices can you do to shift your heart away from disdain towards love?

Prayer

Loving Creator, you have formed us in love and crafted us in your image. You look on us and you love us. Help us look on others and love them when it is difficult. Whether it is something petty or something important, let us love. Make us into wholly loving people. May the grace of our Lord Jesus Christ, the love of God, and the fellowship of the Holy Spirit be with us. Amen.

Value

"There are none in the humanly 'down' position so low that they cannot be lifted up by entering God's order, and none in the humanly 'up' position so high that they can disregard God's point of view on their lives." (DC 89)

"Be assured, the wicked will not go unpunished, but those who are righteous will escape." Proverbs 11:21

As we live in 21st century America, we find ourselves in a complex social environment. Though many would like to describe our country as "Christian," one need not look very close to see that the values which govern our society are not Christian. In fact, if we look closely, we would see that they are entirely antithetical to God's Kingdom. Jesus' message was a simple one—God's rule on Earth had come in himself.

Now that Jesus was walking among us, the world has changed. We see in Jesus the very face of him who created and loves us. We witness the sick being healed, the blind's sight restored, and the deaf hearing. We see lives of destruction be wrought into holiness and purity by a simple act of love. In all, God's Kingdom is entirely foreign to America's. The kingdom of red, white, and blue would rather determine one's value through tangible means; that is, through their social and economic position. If one has wealth, we grant them a higher status. Fancy car? Even higher. Large house? Diversified stock holdings? Extravagant vacation? The list could go on, but the point remains—our worth is tied to the things of this world. The difficulty of this value system lies in its reliance upon chance.

Hard work has allowed some to gain wealth, but in the vast amount of cases, wealth is tethered to one's position at birth. We cannot choose where, when, and to whom we are born, thus using this as a measure of value is fallacious. The poor, not by their own choosing, are subject to a lower status simply due to chance. If, however, we choose to view the world as God's Kingdom, as Jesus did, we discover a whole new value system in place, one that is rooted in God's loving disposition towards us. In God's Kingdom, the wealthy are under his domain just as the poor, they are not favored over those in poverty, rather God loves all equally. The 'up' are brought down as the 'down' are raised up, each to their proper status before their loving Creator.

Questions for Understanding

How do you make value judgments? Is it more akin to God's way or our culture's?

In what ways are you 'down' and in need up raising, or 'up' and in need of humbling?

Prayer

O Divine Savior, we thank you for your love for us and your willingness to allow us into your family. Let us live in your love, deliver us from the ways of this world and bring us into your way of life. Let us see our neighbor not as the world prescribes but as you do. Give us the courage to imitate you, O Lord, in the face of a world who is against your ways. Divorce us from our biases and preconceived notions and draw us into your love. Amen.

Judge Not

"This is what Jesus means when he says, "Judge not." He is telling us that we should, and that we can become the kind of person who does not condemn or blame others. As we do so, the power of God's kingdom will be more freely available to bless and guide those around us into his ways." (DC 217-218)

"Or how can you say to your neighbor, "Let me take the speck out of your eye," while the log is in your own eye? You hypocrite, first take the log out of your own eye, and then you will see clearly to take the speck out of your neighbor's eye." Matthew 7:4-5

We often use the practice of condemnation as a vehicle to correct other people's wrong practices. While we may think we are trying to help, we do the opposite and hurt our witness at the same time. Condemnation is exclusion. In condemning someone we say that they are unworthy of life and are irredeemable. The kingdom is inclusive, for "while we were still sinners Christ died for us" (Rom 5:8).

Who then is to correct others? "Correction is reserved for those who live and work in a divine power not their own" (DC 219). Correction is about restoration not condemnation. When we seek to correct our brothers and sisters, we need to feel the weight of their burden so that we rid ourselves of any sense of pride. Never should we approach a friend and seek to correct them with an ounce of pride still within us. Any attempt at correction with pride in our hearts is self-serving.

The kingdom of God is available to all, and our prideful attempts to correct others leads to condemnation. This is what Jesus meant when he told us to first "take the log out of [our] own eye." Rid ourselves of condemnation so that we can work toward the restoration of our fallen brothers and sisters.

Questions for Understanding

What are your honest intentions when you ask someone to change? Is it self-serving?

How do you rid yourself of condemnation when you seek to correct?

Prayer

Redeeming Christ, thank you for opening the kingdom of heaven to a sinner like me. I pray that you would use me as a vessel for the restoration of those with whom I will interact today. Rid me of any self-righteousness and condemnation in order for your name to be glorified. I pray this in the name of my king who has delivered me, Jesus Christ. Amen.

Letting Go

"What we are actually doing with our proper condemnation and our wonderful solutions, more often than not, is taking others out of their own responsibility and out of God's hands and trying to bring them under our control." (DC 230)

"No one has power over the wind to restrain the wind, or power over the day of death." (Ecclesiastes 8:8)

In reply to the inquiring scribe, Jesus commanded that we are to love our neighbors as ourselves. This along with Love of God is the greatest commandment encapsulating all others. The so-called "golden rule" has served as the basis of moral thinking for millennia, yet despite the maxim's prevalence few live in such a manner. In fact, if asked what this rule means, many, I think, would be unable to provide an adequate account.

So, we must ask "what does it actually mean to love our neighbor as our self?" The answer, at least partly, lies in personhood, that is, each individual's capacity to will and have desires of their own. Loving requires a recognition of the other as a person like oneself, without this, the person is relegated to a subhuman status where they become an object that can be manipulated and controlled. When we refuse to acknowledge the other as a person, we fail to love as God loves us.

Even if our manipulation is for what we perceive as good, we fail to love. If we look to God as our example, we see that he requires not simply our obedience, but our willful obedience. The former he could accomplish through his might, the latter only through our assent. God treats us as persons respecting our will and desires. Of course, he desires us to come to him, but he will not force us, to do so would be to lose something essential to love–willful participation.

Questions for Understanding

In what ways do we control people, or are being controlled? How does this affect us and those we love?

How are we to love without control?

Prayer

Tender Father, we thank you for your gentleness towards us in that you patiently wait and beckon us to come to you. You would rather wait eternally than force our love. We ask, Lord, that you would teach us to love as you do, that we may see in our neighbor their unique personhood as something to be cherished and not controlled. We pray for the wisdom to love without manipulation. Amen.

The Discipline of Secrecy

"In both avoiding evil and doing good, our respect should be for God alone. We may think it is okay to avoid evil for fear of being seen, for in any case we do avoid the evil. But that only shows we have no respect for God and would disobey him but for the opinions of others. The basic principle is the same in both cases. The discipline of secrecy will help us break the grip of human opinion over our souls and out actions." (DC 200)

"But when you give alms, do not let your left hand know what your right hand is doing, so that your alms may be done in secret; and your Father who sees in secret will reward you." Matthew 6:3-4

We have enslaved ourselves to the people around us. Social media is driven by "likes" and "followers" constantly pushing us to gain the approval of others. We no longer take pictures in order to save memories but to share them with others, purely to impress. The push to make our lives exciting or look as though we have everything together continues to increase, yet countless studies show that depression in the United States is rising.

The discipline of secrecy is our God-given tool to combat our enslavement to the opinions of others. So much of sin is rooted in our attempts to manipulate the way which other people think of us. When we practice secrecy are we doing so with the intention to shut people out? Certainly not! We are called to be hospitable people. Secrecy allows us to put the opinions of others entirely in God's hand.

How often do we excitedly post a picture online from that day's service project? We wait and get excited to check who all liked the good work we did. In doing so we are manipulating other people. Serve in secret and allow God to determine if and when our deeds are noticed. In doing this, we demonstrate the trust we have in our heavenly Father.

Questions for Understanding

How do you attempt to manipulate the way others think about you?

How would your social media profile look if you were to pray about your motives in posting prior to doing so?

Prayer

Faithful Father, with whom we have entrusted our whole lives, we thank you that you concern yourself with us. Move our hearts that we may focus on doing what is right in your eyes, not to gain the favor of others, but to be faithful servants to our savior. Through Jesus Christ who guides our lives, Amen.

The Discipline of Restorative Love

"By truly loving our adversary, we stand within the reality of God's kingdom and resources, and it is very likely we will draw our adversary into it also." (DC 157)

"You have heard that it was said, 'You shall love your neighbor and hate your enemy.' But I say to you, love your enemies and pray for those who persecute you." Matthew 5:43-44

The Amish are often the punchlines of jokes, even from within Christian circles. But in 2006, these separatists demonstrated to the church and the world what the kingdom of God looked like. In October, a man opened fire inside of an Amish school for girls. He shot eight girls, five of whom died. He then took his own life.

The pain that this community must have felt is unimaginable. But even though they felt intense pain, they did not allow their pain to mutate into hatred. Although the perpetrator was dead, the Amish loved their enemy by loving his family. They took care of the shooter's widow, parents, and in-laws in their difficult time. They did not even permit themselves to speak ill of the man who had shed innocent blood.

Jesus describes a new, kingdom way of living in the world, and this Amish community followed his example.

Jesus' way calls us to be present with enemies; actively showing them the same incarnational love that Jesus has for us, them, and the people who crucified him. There should be no distinction in how I interact with an enemy and how I interact with my closest friends because both are individuals made in God's image. Be present with them unless being around them threatened your wellbeing. If it would be harmful, practicing love could mean praying for them and asking God to bless them, transform them, or exact justice upon them so that they would be led to repentance.

How we treat people reflects how they view our King, so when we love our enemies, they feel and know the love of Christ. When they are drawn in, they become brothers and sisters. Only the transformative love of Christ can turn enemies into siblings.

Questions for Understanding

Who are those people you consider enemies or adversaries?

How can you go out of your way to show them the love of God?

Prayer

Almighty God, we praise you because you are just, and you promise to repay evil. Help us trust in your promise. Help us also show the same kind of delivering love that you constantly show to us. Where there is hate, help us sow love. May the peace of God, which surpasses all understanding fill our lives so that we can love our enemies. In the name of the Father, the Son, and the Holy Spirit we pray. Amen.

Just as You Are

"He teaches us that he accepts us. He doesn't just deal with us in terms of what we do or don't do. But he deals with us in terms of who we are. And I see in his love and his death on the cross and his acceptance, not of my facade, but of the real me." (BDW 182)

"But God proves his love for us in that while we still were sinners Christ died for us." Romans 5:8

He accepts us. We do not have to perform to earn his love. We do not have to practice the spiritual disciplines perfectly to earn his acceptance. C.H. Spurgeon said, "At this day God loves us, and he will love us forever. He loves us infinitely, and he could not love us more than that if we had never fallen."[3]

His acceptance of us is the motivation to change. When we understand that he accepts us, we grow in our love for him. And the reciprocal love between God and us is what initiates the transformation. If he did not accept our authentic selves, we would never be able to change. His acceptance comes before our transformation. Brennan Manning writes, "God never says to us, 'I want you to be something else' without saying, 'I love you as you are.'"[4] This may seem like a contradicting statement, but he does not call us to change so that he will love us, but because he loves us.

And when we understand that he accepts us, we can change. If we do not think he accepts us we will try to be good enough and when we find out we can't, we will get discouraged and give up. That's why we can't allow ourselves to build facades but instead we must turn our eyes upon Jesus and see the love that he has for us demonstrated by his life, death, and resurrection.

Do not be discouraged if you think you will never be spiritual enough for God. He accepts you; however, do not take this as an excuse to ignore his call to become more like him. Pursue Christlikeness today.

Questions for Understanding

Do you find yourself trying to earn God's acceptance?

What can you do to remind yourself that God accepts you and always will?

Prayer

O God, you are the infinite creator who possesses all power and glory, yet you condescend to call us friends. Help us experience the depths of your love and let us be transformed by it. So that we may be shaped by your love instead of striving to earn it. In the name of the Father and the Son and the Holy Spirit we pray. Amen.

Bibliography

BDW - Gary W. Moon, *Becoming Dallas Willard: The Formation of a Philosopher, Teacher, and Christ Follower* (InterVarsity Press, 2018);

HG - Dallas Willard, *Hearing God: Developing a Conversational Relationship with God* (InterVarsity Press, 1999);

RH - Dallas Willard, *Renovation of the Heart: Putting On the Character of Christ* (Tyndale House, 2014);

DC - Dallas Willard, *The Divine Conspiracy: Rediscovering Our Hidden Life In God* (Harper Collins, 2009);

GO - Dallas Willard, *The Great Omission: Reclaiming Jesus's Essential Teachings on Discipleship* (Zondervan, 2006);

SD - Dallas Willard, *The Spirit of the Disciplines: Understanding How God Changes Lives* (Harper Collins, 2009).

The Holy Bible: New Revised Standard Version. 1989. Nashville: Thomas Nelson Publishers.

End-notes

---

[1] Francis Thompson, *The Hound of Heaven and Other Poems* (Branden Books, 1978). p. 78.

[2] Gregory A. Boyd, *Present Perfect: Finding God in the Now* (Zondervan, 2010). pp. 18-22.

[3] CH Spurgeon. "Plenary Absolution." (Sermon 1108, MTP 19:235)

[4] Gregory A. Boyd, *Present Perfect: Finding God in the Now* (Zondervan, 2010). p. 88.

Printed in Great Britain
by Amazon